THE NEW WEATHER

THE CLIMATE SYSTEM

HEATHER PIDCOCK-REED

THE NEW WEATHER

AMAZING WEATHER FACTS
CLIMATE AND WEATHER
THE CLIMATE SYSTEM
EXTREME WEATHER
WHAT IS WEATHER?

THE NEW WEATHER

THE CLIMATE SYSTEM

HEATHER PIDCOCK-REED

MASON CREST
MIAMI

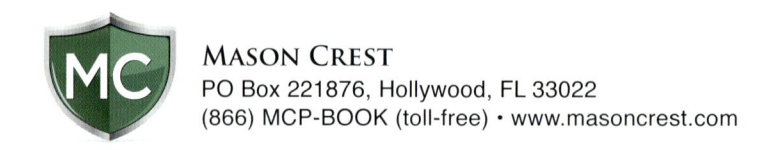

MASON CREST
PO Box 221876, Hollywood, FL 33022
(866) MCP-BOOK (toll-free) • www.masoncrest.com

Copyright © 2023 by Mason Crest, an imprint of National Highlights, Inc. All rights reserved. No part of this publication may be reproduced or transmitted in any form or by any means, electronic or mechanical, including photocopying, recording, taping, or any information storage and retrieval system, without permission in writing from the publisher.

Printed in the United States of America

First printing
9 8 7 6 5 4 3 2 1

Series ISBN: 978-1-4222-4560-6
Hardcover ISBN: 978-1-4222-4561-3
ebook ISBN: 978-1-4222-7248-0

Cataloging-in-Publication Data on file with the Library of Congress

Developed and Produced by National Highlights, Inc.
Editor: Jacqueline Havelka - Inform Scientific
Cover and Interior Design by Torque Advertising+Design
Layout: Priceless Digital Media, LLC

Publisher's Note: Websites listed in this book were active at the time of publication. The publisher is not responsible for websites that have changed their address or discontinued operation since the date of publication. The publisher reviews and updates the websites each time the book is reprinted.

QR CODES AND LINKS TO THIRD-PARTY CONTENT

You may gain access to certain third-party content ("Third-Party Sites") by scanning and using the QR Codes that appear in this publication (the "QR Codes"). We do not operate or control in any respect any information, products, or services on such Third-Party Sites linked to by us via the QR Codes included in this publication, and we assume no responsibility for any materials you may access using the QR Codes. Your use of the QR Codes may be subject to terms, limitations, or restrictions set forth in the applicable terms of use or otherwise established by the owners of the Third-Party Sites. Our linking to such Third-Party Sites via the QR Codes does not imply an endorsement or sponsorship of such Third-Party Sites or the information, products, or services offered on or through the Third-Party Sites, nor does it imply an endorsement or sponsorship of this publication by the owners of such Third-Party Sites.

CONTENTS

Chapter 1: Atmosphere 7
Chapter 2: Biosphere 19
Chapter 3: Ice 35
Chapter 4: Land 47
Chapter 5: Ocean 61
Series Glossary of Key Terms 72
Further Reading and Internet Resources 74
Organizations to Contact 76
Index 77
Author's Biography and Photo Credits 80

KEY ICONS TO LOOK FOR:

Words to Understand: These words with their easy-to-understand definitions will increase the reader's understanding of the text while building vocabulary skills.

Sidebars: This boxed material within the main text allows readers to build knowledge, gain insights, explore possibilities, and broaden their perspectives by weaving together additional information to provide realistic and holistic perspectives.

Educational Videos: Readers can view videos by scanning our QR codes, providing them with additional educational content to supplement the text. Examples include news coverage, moments in history, speeches, iconic sports moments, and much more!

Text-Dependent Questions: These questions send the reader back to the text for more careful attention to the evidence presented there.

Research Projects: Readers are pointed toward areas of further inquiry connected to each chapter. Suggestions are provided for projects that encourage deeper research and analysis.

Series Glossary of Key Terms: This back-of-the-book glossary contains terminology used throughout this series. Words found here increase the reader's ability to read and comprehend higher-level books and articles in this field.

WORDS TO UNDERSTAND

jet stream: a fast flowing, narrow, meandering river of wind in the earth's atmosphere

precipitation: a term describing any form of liquid falling from the sky, such as rain, sleet, snow, or hail

sea level: the average height of the ocean's surface

ultraviolet (UV) radiation: a type of electromagnetic radiation that is present in sunlight

CHAPTER 1

ATMOSPHERE

Weather and climate are important parts of our daily lives. They impact decisions we make, such as what we're going to wear for the day and what activities we're going to participate in. Weather has to do with the current conditions within the earth's atmosphere in a local area. Look out the window right now and you'll see an example of weather. Climate has to do with long-term weather patterns in an area. For example, areas that are considered to be desert climates have established patterns of low **precipitation**.

While climate covers a long-term interval, it can still change. In fact, many scientists think the earth is currently experiencing a period of global warming. Changes in climate have consistently happened throughout the earth's lengthy history, and typically take thousands and even millions of years to occur. However, the majority of climate scientists today believe that our current warming period is moving at a faster pace than what has happened in the past. These scientists believe that these changes in our climate are occurring because of human activities.

The gases that surround the earth make up the atmosphere. From space, astronauts looking back on Earth call it the thin blue line.

To truly understand the impact of climate change on the earth, we need to have an understanding of the climate system. Weather and climate are interconnected parts of the earth's climate system, which is a complex system of interrelated parts that work together to create the weather. There are five elements to the climate system: the air (atmosphere), all the living things on Earth (biosphere), ice (cryosphere), land (lithosphere), and oceans (hydrosphere).

The Atmosphere

The mixture of different gases that surround the earth is called the *atmosphere*. Without an atmosphere, life on Earth would not be possible. The atmosphere serves several functions. It gives us air to breathe, protects us from the **ultraviolet (UV) radiation** that comes from our sun, and keeps our planet at the temperatures necessary to sustain life. All of the other planets in our solar system, as well as a handful of moons, have some sort of atmosphere. The earth's unique atmosphere is the only one that is suitable for life.

The earth's atmosphere is made up of multiple levels, each of which has a specific trait and function. The six layers of the atmosphere are known as the:

- **Troposphere**
- **Stratosphere**
- **Mesosphere**
- **Thermosphere**
- **Exosphere**
- **Ionosphere**

Troposphere: The troposphere is the lowest layer of the earth's atmosphere. It begins at ground level and extends to around 33,000 feet (approximately 10 km) above **sea level**. The troposphere is where we live, and it is also where almost all of the earth's weather happens. Since 99 percent of all of the water vapor found inside the atmosphere is found within this layer, it's where most clouds form. The air at the bottom of the troposphere is warm and grows colder the higher up you go. In addition to this phenomenon, the higher you go in the troposphere, the lower the air pressure is.

THE POWER OF SOLAR RADIATION

The energy from our sun provides the earth with the light and warmth required for life. But did you know that we can harness that energy to turn it into the type of power that makes our modern societies work properly? Solar power is a renewable energy source that can provide us with heat and electricity for our homes and businesses.

Vast swaths of land could be used to harness the sun's energy. Pictured here is a huge field of solar power arrays.

Stratosphere: The second layer of the atmosphere is known as the *stratosphere*. This starts at the top of the troposphere, around 31 miles (50 km) above the surface of the earth. The higher you go within the stratosphere, the warmer it gets! That is because the ozone layer is a part of the stratosphere. This warmer air also means that there is less turbulence within the air, which is why passenger planes fly in the lower levels of the stratosphere. The **jet stream** is also present in the area bordering the troposphere and the stratosphere.

Mesosphere: Located around 53 miles (85.3 km) above the surface of the earth, the mesosphere is the next layer of the atmosphere. Temperatures once again get colder the higher up you go within the mesosphere. The air pressure is also so low that you can't breathe the air in this layer. The mesosphere is where most of the meteors that enter the earth's atmosphere burn up.

Thermosphere: The next level is called the thermosphere. The thermosphere is located approximately 311–621 miles (500 to 1,000 km) above the earth's surface. This is the layer that absorbs UV radiation and X-rays from the sun. Even though this area of the atmosphere absorbs heat, the air is so thin that it's freezing cold. The thermosphere is where most of our satellites orbit the earth. This is also the area where the aurora borealis (the northern and southern lights) occur.

Exosphere: The exosphere is the next layer that comprises the earth's atmosphere. This layer is located between 62,000–120,000 miles (99,799 to 193,121 km) above the earth. This layer is considered by many experts to be the last section between the earth's atmosphere and outer space. The air in the exosphere is incredibly thin—so thin that some of the air from the atmosphere is always leaking slowly out into space.

Learn all about what causes aurora borealis in this short video.

Ionosphere: While the ionosphere is not a separate, distinct layer like the others, it is a series of regions existing within and between the mesosphere and thermosphere. These areas contain large levels of electrically charged atoms and molecules that have been created by solar radiation. This section is constantly growing and shrinking, based on the amount of energy that it is absorbing from our sun. The ionosphere plays an important role when it comes to communication and navigation systems. This is the area of the atmosphere that our radio and GPS signals travel through.

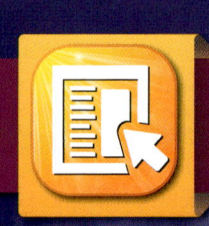

SMOG

If you live in a city, you've probably experienced smog before. In simple terms, smog is a hazy substance in the air that reduces visibility. Smog, a combination of the words "smoke" and "fog," is caused by polluted air. It forms when ozone gases mix with air pollution. Smog is dangerous to humans, animals, and plants. It can make it difficult to breathe, and it also contributes to the development of heart and lung diseases.

Many large cities around the world have smog. The polluted air can reduce visibility and cause breathing issues.

The Ozone

Ozone is a reactive gas that is made up of three types of oxygen atoms. It occurs within both the stratosphere (the upper atmosphere) and the troposphere (the lower atmosphere). It is both natural and man-made. It is formed naturally inside of the stratosphere when UV radiation from the sun interacts with molecular oxygen, which reduces the levels of radiation that reach the surface of the earth. Ground-level ozone is present in the air that we breathe. It is formed when two different kinds of air pollutants combine and interact. These reactions between pollutants tend to be higher in locations where temperatures are higher. This is one of the contributing factors toward the development of smog or haze in areas where there is a lot of air pollution.

Studying the Ozone Layer

The ozone layer is considered to be a part of the stratosphere. This thin strata is located around 6–30 miles (9.6 to 48.2 km) above the surface of the earth. It is comprised of trace gases that absorb most of the radiation from the sun that hits our planet. While part of this radiation is what gives us the light and warm temperatures necessary to stay alive, in large doses, it can be harmful.

One type of radiation that the ozone layer protects us from is known as *UV (ultraviolet) light*. Too much UV light can break through the protective layers of living organisms (such as skin), causing damage to the DNA molecules existing within animals and plants. Too much UV light will kill vegetation and destroy sensitive ecosystems.

Look at this ozone hole as seen from space! The hole forms when UV light destroys a section of the stratosphere.

THE HOLE IN THE OZONE

Did you know that there is an ozone hole that forms over Antarctica during certain times of the year? This ozone hole forms because of the composition of the stratosphere in this region. The conditions present in the south polar stratosphere are the most favorable conditions for ozone destruction to occur. Since the climate during the winter in this area is so cold, clouds form in the stratosphere. Once spring comes, the sun's UV rays hit this region and begin the process of destroying the ozone. This process happens until the stratospheric clouds have disappeared due to warming temperatures. During the summer, the lack of these clouds allows for the ozone layer to be replenished. High concentrations of ODS in the ozone lead to this seasonal hole becoming larger.

During the late 1970s, experts noticed that the amount of ozone existing in the atmosphere was beginning to decrease. This reduction was mostly attributed to harmful manufactured chemicals that were being released into the air. These chemicals are referred to as *ozone-depleting substances (ODS)*. These ODS wind up inside the stratosphere, where they release atoms that begin to break down the ozone, turning it into oxygen. This has created a depletion in the ozone, as well as a hole in the ozone.

Since radiation from the sun is so dangerous, the role that the ozone layer plays in filtering out much of that radiation is a critical one. To put it simply, the ozone layer functions as a sort of shield for everything that lives on Earth. Without it, there would be no life present on Earth.

How Does CO_2 Contribute to the Atmosphere?

Carbon dioxide (CO_2) is an important greenhouse gas that is present within the earth's atmosphere. This gas both absorbs heat and then slowly releases it over time. Without this process, our planet would not stay warm enough for life to be present.

Over the lengthy history of our planet, the earth has experienced many natural increases in carbon dioxide within the atmosphere. This has led to different warming periods that signaled the end of various ice ages that our planet has experienced.

As mentioned earlier, our planet appears to be currently undergoing a warming period. While there have been naturally occurring warming periods within the history of the earth, the current scientific consensus is that this change is occurring due to human activities. CO_2 emissions from human technologies—especially burning fossil fuels like coal and oil to generate power—have led to a rapid increase in the amounts of carbon dioxide levels within the atmosphere, which has caused temperatures to begin rising across the planet. These documented changes have led scientists to believe that our current experience of global warming and climate changes have been primarily caused by humans.

TEXT-DEPENDENT QUESTIONS

1. List the six layers of the earth's atmosphere.
2. What is the purpose of the ozone layer?
3. How does carbon dioxide work within the earth's atmosphere?

RESEARCH PROJECT

The atmosphere is an important component of our planet's climate system. Use the Internet to conduct research on the different layers of the atmosphere. Find out at what height each layer is located, as well as what the air pressure and temperature are in each layer. After you've collected your information, create a poster, flip book, or 3-D model of the earth and the different layers of the atmosphere. Be sure to include the data you gathered during your research, and share it with your science class or weather club.

WORDS TO UNDERSTAND

biomes: the types of animals and plants that live within a particular habitat
ecosystems: localized communities of organisms that interact amongst themselves and their physical environments
extinction: the elimination of a species, family, or other group of plant or animal from existence
natural habitat: an environmental area where a specific species lives and calls home

CHAPTER 2

BIOSPHERE

Earth is an amazingly diverse place. Our planet features oceans, forests, deserts, mountains, plains, and rain forests. That diversity also exists within the different types of life forms found on Earth. Our planet also hosts an abundance of plants and animals that have evolved over time to live in unique places. These locations and living beings have been deeply shaped by the earth's climate system.

What is the Biosphere?

Also known as the *ecosphere*, the biosphere is the part of the climate system that comprises all of the parts of the planet where life exists. It not only consists of the plants and animals living on the planet, but it is also made up of the earth's crust, water, atmospheric gas, and light. The earth's biosphere is the only known place where life exists within our universe.

The area considered to be the biosphere covers ground, air, and water. While the biosphere is measured to be around 12 miles (19.3 km) from the top to bottom, nearly all life on the planet lives in a specific region between 1,640 feet (500 m) under the ocean's surface to approximately 3.75 miles (6 km) above sea level. It consists of many different **ecosystems**, which can be further broken down into **biomes**. There are six primary kinds of biomes (each of which are intimately shaped by weather and climate). They are:

- **Tundras**
- **Prairies**
- **Deserts**
- **Tropical Rain Forests**
- **Deciduous Forests**
- **Oceans**

Tundras: Tundras are a type of biome consisting of a climate that has colder temperatures and short growing seasons. These areas are characterized by a lack of trees, vegetation that is low to the ground, and harsh weather conditions.

This incredible picture is of the Alaskan tundra. These biomes exist in colder temperatures and have a characteristic lack of trees.

Horses graze on a natural prairie. This biome type has few trees and extensive grassland.

Prairies: These biomes consist of large stretches of flat grassland with few trees. Prairies also have moderate rainfall and moderate temperatures, so such areas are excellent for agriculture.

Deserts: A desert biome doesn't receive a lot of precipitation. Most of us correlate a desert with having sand, but the general consensus amongst experts is that a desert is any land area that gets no more than 10 inches (25.4 cm) of precipitation in a year.

The Antarctic Desert is the biggest desert in the world, covering all of the land of Antarctica—the continent located over the South Pole. Antarctica is also the coldest place on Earth. The temperature in the winter is cold enough to freeze water year round. The temperature in the middle of Antarctica is much colder than the temperature on the coasts. Antarctica has two seasons: summer and winter. Earth is tilted in space and the direction of tilt never changes. During summer, Antarctica is on the side of Earth tilted toward the sun. It is always sunny. In winter, Antarctica is on the side of Earth tilted away from the sun. Then, the continent is always dark. The

Biosphere

desert has no trees or bushes, and the only plants that can survive the extreme cold temperatures are algae and mosses.

Tropical rain forests: This area of tall trees receives large amounts of rainfall. Rain forests are some of our planet's oldest living ecosystems and play an important role in regulating our climate.

Deciduous Forests: A deciduous forest has trees that drop their leaves in one season. They are characterized by temperate climates, with winter seasons, and precipitation occurring all year long.

Oceans: The ocean biome is the largest found on the planet, as it covers approximately 70 percent of the earth's surface. The ocean plays a very important role in our climate system.

As you can see, the biosphere is an incredibly complex system of interrelated parts. Many of these components have important roles to play when it comes to our climate system. Some are natural effects, while others are caused by the actions of humans and technology.

The Role of the Biosphere in Our Climate System

Plants have an important role to play within our climate system. During the process of photosynthesis, plants take in carbon dioxide and water from the atmosphere and the earth's soil. The plant then coverts the water it has taken in and turns it into oxygen, which is released into the air. Meanwhile, CO2 is converted into glucose molecules, which are then used to store the plant's energy. This process helps to keep climates cooler by reducing the amounts of carbon dioxide that are present within the atmosphere.

The abundance of plant life found within the planet's rain forests play a large part in our climate system. This is because they absorb large amounts of CO_2 from the earth's atmosphere and contribute approximately 20 percent of the world's oxygen, while also absorbing around 20 percent of man-made carbon emissions.

Animals also have an important role that can impact our climate. For example, farm animals produce methane gas as they digest their food, which is then released and absorbed by the

The Amazon rain forest is the largest in the world. It spans over 2.3 million square miles (6 million square kilometers) and is the home to thousands of animal and plant species.

atmosphere. Methane gases contribute to global warming and climate change. This means that large farming operations make a significant impact on greenhouse gas emissions, contributing to global warming trends and climate shifts.

The largest deciduous forest is in the eastern part of North America. By 1850, the area was almost completely deforested to create lumber for housing.

The ocean biome is by far the largest biome of the earth. This biome covers 70 percent of the earth's surface.

Human activity within the biosphere has had an enormous impact on our climate system. Factories, power plants, vehicles, and other human activities release large amounts of carbon dioxide into the earth's atmosphere. In addition, people have an impact on local environments via the destruction of native biomes and ecosystems in order to make room for towns and cities. Agricultural activities can deplete the quality of the soil, which can negatively affect the growth of plants.

ARTIFICIAL BIOSPHERES

Did you know that there have been artificially made biospheres? They're designed to study enclosed ecosystems so that scientists can learn more about how our actual biosphere works. These man-made biospheres contain an array of ecosystems: from deserts, savannahs, and rain forests to marshes and farms. These small-scale models of real-life ecosystems contain plants and animals. Many of the studies conducted within these biospheres have helped us to understand climate change in a better way.

Currently run by the University of Arizona, Biosphere 2 is a great example of an artificial biosphere. It is located in Oracle, Arizona, and was originally constructed between the years 1987 to 1991. It consists of seven biome areas, including a rain forest, an ocean with coral reef, mangrove wetlands, savannah grassland, fog desert, an agricultural system, and a human habitat. It was utilized in closed-system experiments from 1991 to 1993, and again for approximately six months in 1994. While there were many problems during these experiments, subsequent research has allowed for an understanding of the earth's various habitats and their impact on the climate system. You can now attend tours and science camps at Biosphere 2.

Photosynthesis in plants is very important to Earth because it contributes to the oxygen and carbon dioxide cycle that keeps the planet healthy.

How a Biosphere Stays Healthy

Earth's biosphere plays important roles in maintaining the earth's climate and sustaining life. To ensure that our planet can continue sustaining life, we need to be sure that we are taking good care of it. This means managing our resources properly, as well as reducing the number of harmful activities that humans participate in that negatively impact our planet. Land, water, and air management are the best ways to keep our biosphere healthy and sustainable.

Managing our land means conserving **natural habitats** as much as possible. Not only in preserving ecosystems and biomes, such as rain forests and wetlands, but also by encouraging biodiversity—allowing a wide range of plants and animals native to an area to grow and thrive. Another aspect of land management lies in developing sustainable agricultural processes that won't lead to a degradation of native topsoil.

MARS ON EARTH BIOSPHERE

One potentially interesting use of artificial biospheres is to test out ecological habitats that will be used to support human life on other planets. Currently, research is being conducted on how to sustain human life on planets such as Mars. The designs for these habitats will consist of closed life-support systems that allow for the purification of air, the production of food, and the recycling of water and wastewater. They will be able to be used in training future Mars explorers before their missions to Mars take place.

This is an artist's concept of the Mars biosphere. Perhaps one day soon, this incredible station will be on the surface of Mars. Maybe you will be there too as a Mars scientist!

Biosphere

Taking care of our oceans and freshwater systems are included in taking care of our biosphere. This means keeping our water clean and pollution free. In addition, we should be sure that we fish sustainably, meaning releasing immature fish back into rivers and oceans so that they can reproduce and keep water ecosystems intact.

Reducing the amount of air pollution that we emit is one way that we can protect our biosphere. Since human beings are the primary cause of air pollution, we need to ensure that we keep our carbon emissions (as well as other harmful gas and chemical emissions) as low as possible. To accomplish that, we must develop sustainable energy sources that don't harm our environment.

Another way to reduce human impact on the biosphere is to develop our societies in a sustainable way. Encouraging conservation of nature while also carefully monitoring how our activities affect the world around us can help us meet our needs while keeping the planet as healthy as possible. One step is not overhunting or overfishing in an area. Another is avoiding activities that are harmful to natural habitats, such as draining wetlands, as well as the practice of deforestation.

Is Deforestation Contributing to the Destruction of the Biosphere?

Deforestation is the intentional clearing of forests. This is done in order to provide people with room for agricultural pursuits, as well as to provide the inhabitants with wood for fuel, construction, and manufacturing. This practice has significantly impacted landscapes and ecosystems across the globe. For example, approximately 2,000 years ago, 80 percent of Western Europe was covered in forests; today, only 34 percent of the region is forested.

Deforestation is harmful to the biosphere, as it allows more CO_2 to be released into the earth's atmosphere. For example, a common practice in deforestation is to cut and burn the trees in the desired area. Since trees breathe in carbon dioxide, that carbon is locked within their wood. When trees are burned, they release that CO_2 back into the atmosphere. That isn't the only way that deforestation leads to more carbon dioxide in the atmosphere. Fewer trees on the planet means that there are fewer trees to absorb carbon dioxide in general.

Deforestation is causing destruction across our planet. It contributes to soil erosion, CO_2 imbalances, and so much more.

The practice of deforestation also eliminates biodiversity and destroys local ecosystems. Forests teem with all kinds of plant and animal life. When forests are demolished, those plants and animals are also eliminated. Too much deforestation can lead many plant and animal species toward **extinction**. There are many scientists who believe that we are already in the middle of a mass-extinction episode.

In addition, the soil in deforested areas is more prone to erosion, which leads to the forest becoming an open area that is dry rather than one that is closed and wet. The plants that are left within the area are more vulnerable to wildfires. These wildfires in turn are bad for the atmosphere, as they release carbon dioxide into the air. In addition to this, wildfires can cause a great deal of damage to both ecosystems and human habitations.

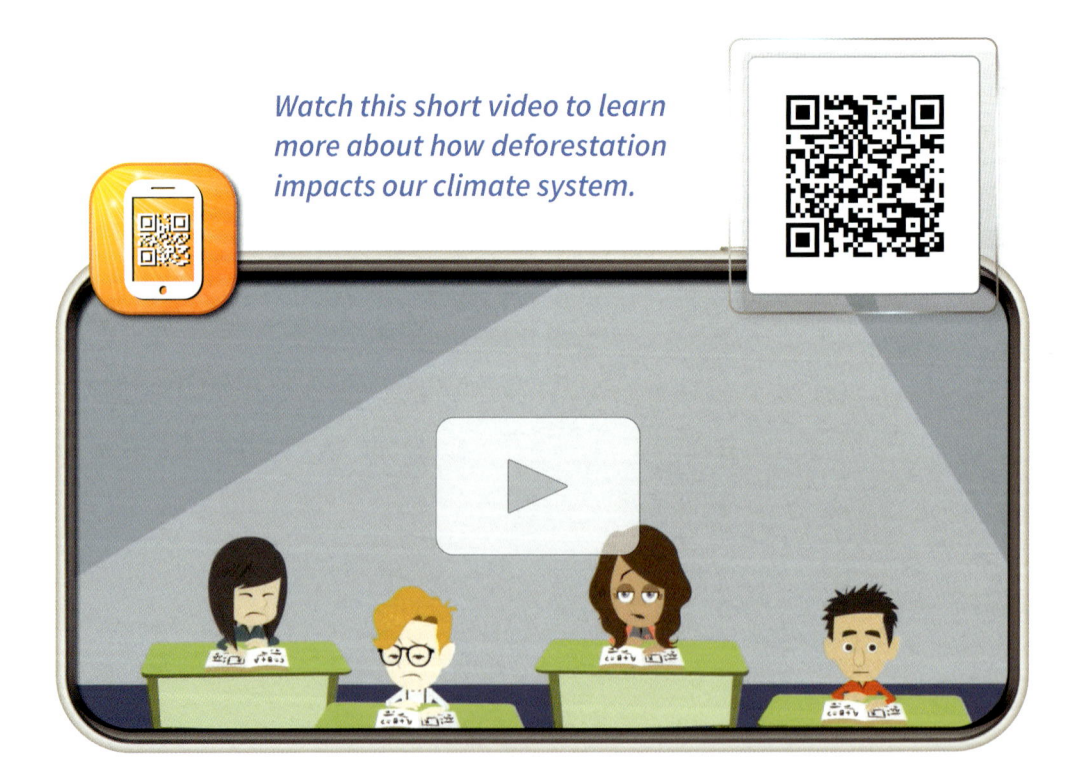

Watch this short video to learn more about how deforestation impacts our climate system.

TEXT-DEPENDENT QUESTIONS

1. What are the six primary types of biomes found within the biosphere?
2. How does photosynthesis contribute to our climate system?
3. In what ways does deforestation destroy the biosphere?

RESEARCH PROJECT

Using the internet, find instructions on making your own biosphere in a bottle. Following those instructions, build your biosphere. Once you've completed it and completely sealed it off, you won't be able to open it. For the next several weeks, take photos and make weekly notes about what is happening in your biosphere. Share your results with your classmates and your teacher.

WORDS TO UNDERSTAND

alpine: relating to high mountains, including living or growing on mountains above the tree line
epoch: the smallest measurement of geological time
humidity: the amount of water vapor that is found in the air
snowpack: the amount of accumulating snow in a season in a mountainous area

CHAPTER 3

ICE

The third component of our planet's climate system is ice, which is also known as the *cryosphere*. This is comprised of all of the parts of our planet that contain frozen water. The cryosphere includes snow and ice on land, ice caps, permafrost, glaciers, and sea ice. These phenomena play an important role in reflecting solar radiation from the sun away from the earth and back into space. This makes it an incredibly important part of our climate system.

When you think about the earth's ice, you probably think about the North and South Poles (also called the Arctic and Antarctic respectively). However, snow and ice are found all over the world, and in many different forms. In addition to the ice found at the Arctic and Antarctic, the cryosphere also includes:

- **Snow**
- **Ice**
- **Sea Ice**
- **Glaciers and Ice Sheets**
- **Ice Shelves and Icebergs**
- **Frozen Ground**

Snow: When there is a combination of high **humidity** levels and temperatures that are below freezing, snow crystals form within the atmosphere. Any precipitation that falls under these conditions falls as snow, rather than rain. Snow is found all around the globe, even at high elevations near the warm equator. Snow reflects the sun's light and impacts our climate.

Ice: Whenever temperatures drop below freezing, water becomes solid. This form of water is known as *ice*, which is the primary ingredient for sea ice, glaciers, icebergs, ice shelves, and frozen ground. Ice can be found all over the world, but it is most common at higher elevations, higher latitudes, and at night. Scientists examine long tubes of ice they drill out of icy places (known as *ice cores*) to learn more about the earth's climate history.

Sea Ice: Sea ice develops when ocean water is cooled to below freezing levels. Most of the planet's sea ice is found within the Arctic and Antarctic Oceans. Sea ice has a large influence on the earth's climate, so recent declines have greatly concerned climate scientists and environmentalists.

Ships often get trapped by sea ice. The ship gets frozen into an ocean passage and it may take months for the ice to thaw.

This incredible glacier is in Iceland. Notice the grooves that indicate many years of ice buildup.

Glaciers and Ice Sheets: A glacier is a thick mass of ice that has built up over many seasons and moves incredibly slowly. Glaciers are a smaller form of continental glaciers, or ice sheets. Glaciers and ice sheets are so large that they shape landscapes as they move. Glaciers and ice sheets also store the majority of the world's fresh water.

Ice Shelves and Icebergs: When ice sheets and glaciers move into the oceans, ice shelves form. These are found mostly in Greenland and Antarctica, as well as in Arctic. An iceberg is a large, floating mass of ice that has broken off from an ice shelf or glacier. Once free, it then drifts around the ocean, moving away until it melts completely.

Frozen Ground: Frozen ground is defined as any kind of rock or soil within which water has frozen. Permafrost is a permanently frozen layer on or underneath Earth's surface. In some areas, the top layer of permafrost melts during the warm period, but underneath, it remains frozen. Most of the frozen ground on Earth is found in the Arctic and Antarctic, but it is also present at high elevations. One of its functions is to store greenhouse gases.

The History of Ice Ages

As discussed earlier, the earth has had many different warming and cooling periods throughout its long history. An ice age is a lengthy period of time where the earth experiences reduced temperatures, both on its surface and within the atmosphere. This period causes an expansion of polar ice sheets and **alpine** glaciers. Over the past three billion years, the earth has experienced at least five significant ice ages:

- **Huronian (2.4–2.1 billion years ago)**
- **Cryogenian (850–635 million years ago)**
- **Andean-Saharan (460–430 million years ago)**
- **Karoo (360–260 million years ago ago)**
- **Quaternary (2.6 million years ago–present)**

The most recent ice age is the one that occurred just before our current era (known as the interglacial Holocene **epoch**) began around 11,500 years ago. Interglacial periods are warmer intervals of time in between ice ages, when the planet warms and thaws out. The warmer temperatures cause glaciers to melt and sea levels to rise. The warming that ended the last ice age allowed early humanity to flourish. It also led to the abundance of plant and animal life that we see on our planet today.

No one knows exactly how long we can expect our current interglacial period to last. Historically speaking, glacial periods

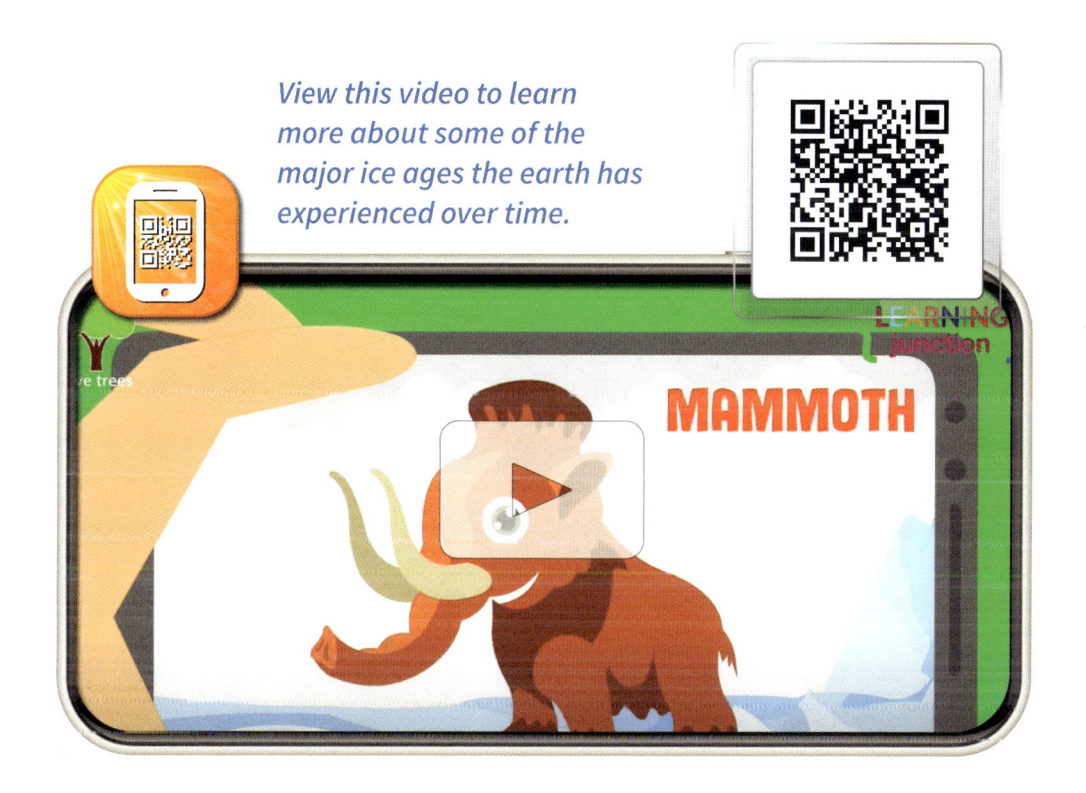

View this video to learn more about some of the major ice ages the earth has experienced over time.

tend to last between 70,000 to 90,000 years, while interglacial periods have only lasted anywhere between 10,000 and 20,000 years. Therefore, we can probably expect our current period to last about as long.

How Much Ice Does the Earth Currently Have?

According to the National Snow and Ice Data Center, 10 percent of the earth's land area is covered by glacial ice, including ice caps, glaciers, and the ice sheets of Antarctica and Greenland. Over 99 percent of ice in the world is contained within these sources. The rest of the planet's ice is contained within permafrost, seasonal snow cover, frozen lakes and rivers, etc.

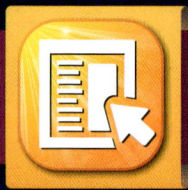

THE GEOLOGIC TIME SCALE

ERA		PERIOD	LIFE FORMS
CENOZOIC	2,6	QUATENARY	
	2,3	NEOGENE	
	66	PALEOGENE	
MESOZOIC	145	CRETACEOUS	
	200	JURASSIC	
	252	TRIASSIC	
PALEOZOIC	300	PERMIAN	
	360	CARBONIFEROUS	
	420	DEVONIAN	
	443	SILURIAN	
	485	ORDOVICIAN	
	544	CAMBRIAN	
	4,6 billion years ago	PRECAMBRIAN	

MILLIONS OF YEARS AGO

The Geological Time Scale is a sort of calendar for events within the geological history of Earth. Within the scale, time is divided into eons, eras, periods, subperiods, epochs, and ages. These time units are defined by the composition of rock strata within sedimentary rocks, igneous rocks, and metamorphic rocks. Fossils are also used to determine different periods.

The New Weather: The Climate System

This incredible view shows an aerial view of Iceland. About 10 percent of Earth's land area is covered in glacial ice.

What Do Ice Formations Tell Us About the Earth's Health?

Scientists use ice to tell them about the history of the earth, which can be helpful in providing them with clues about how climate change worked in the past. The earth's cryosphere provides scientists with a great deal of information regarding how healthy our planet is.

Ice cores pulled out of Earth's ice contain bubbles that have collected the concentration of gases in the atmosphere. This can provide scientists with the information that they need to determine what the composition of the earth's atmosphere was like thousands of years ago. This is how scientists have an idea of what the climate was like long before human beings evolved.

As the earth's climate continues to warm, climate scientists are growing increasingly concerned about melting ice, because the planet's ice helps to reflect the sun's radiation away from the planet. The less ice that the earth has, the warmer the planet will continue to become. In addition, the loss of the planet's ice will also result in the loss of habitats for animals like polar bears, seals, walruses, wolves, and other Arctic species.

Is the Earth Gaining or Losing Ice?

The general consensus amongst scientists is that the earth's ice is melting at a rapid rate. However, in 2015 a group of scientists from NASA published findings that Antarctica was gaining ice rather than losing it. This study caused a lot of controversy, and further studies have indicated that that while the eastern part of the continent had experienced more snowfall, the amount of melting ice from the western part of the continent counteracted this. In addition, the large amounts of ice melting in the Arctic also offsets any gains found in the Antarctic.

Despite the controversial findings of the study, it is evident that the earth's ice is melting. Since 1979, our satellites have shown every year that the amount of ice continues to grow smaller and thinner every season. In fact, in September of 2020, the area of ice in the Arctic was the second smallest that it has ever been since they began recording it. This decrease can be directly attributed to the warming temperatures across the globe.

Changing Ice on Earth

The polar ice caps aren't the only types of ice that are melting. Glaciers located across the United States of America and around the world have been shrinking since the 1960s. And alarmingly, the speed at which glaciers are melting has risen drastically within the past ten years. In addition to this, lakes and rivers are freezing later

SEA ICE AND RISING SEA LEVELS

While sea ice is also melting at an alarming rate, it is not contributing to rising sea levels. This is because sea ice is frozen ocean water, comprised of saltwater and formed from the water that is already in the ocean. When it melts, it doesn't contribute to rising sea levels. The real danger, when it comes to rising sea levels, is from melting freshwater land ice, such as glaciers.

Ice

in the season and thawing earlier when compared with freezes and thaws from earlier time periods.

Another way that ice has changed is in the amount of snowfall that occurs across the world. For example, the total amount of snowfall in the United States has decreased in recent years. While the amounts of snow that any given location receives vary from year to year, the amount of snow cover in North America has decreased at a rate of approximately 1,870 miles (3,009 km) per year. Less snow also means that the **snowpack** around the United States is lighter, which affects our water supplies.

All of the melting land-based ice is also contributing to rising sea levels. And as temperatures across the globe increase, glaciers and other types of ice dissolve at a faster rate. The resulting water then travels through rivers and winds up in the ocean, causing sea levels to rise. According to the United States Geological Survey, if all of the glaciers and ice caps on the earth were to melt, the sea levels would rise around 230 feet (70 m). Every coastal city in the world would flood.

The Antarctic Station for Research

The Antarctic provides us with valuable insights into what is going on with our climate. As of 2022, there are seventy permanent research stations across the continent that represent twenty-nine countries. The United States has its own research base, called the McMurdo Station, and it is the largest presence on the continent.

TEXT-DEPENDENT QUESTIONS

1. List the six types of ice that comprise the earth's cryosphere.
2. How many major ice ages has the earth experienced?
3. How much ice covers the earth?

RESEARCH PROJECT

One of the ways that ice is changing on our planet is through the amount of snowfall that occurs every year. Using the Internet, document average snowfall amounts in your area over the past thirty years. Create a chart showing your findings. Then, write a paragraph explaining what you found. Did your area experience an overall increase or decrease in snowfall? Share your information with your science class or weather club.

WORDS TO UNDERSTAND

crust: the outmost layer of the earth that is made up of different kinds of rocks

drought: a prolonged dry period that can cause extensive crop damage and limit drinking water for humans and animals

lava: molten rock ejected from a volcano during an eruption; the same name is applied to the rock when cooled and hardened

plate tectonics: a theory accepted by the scientific community that states that the earth is made of giant slabs of solid rock that move slowly and change the structure of the earth

CHAPTER 4

LAND

The earth's land is the fourth element of our climate system. Also known as the *lithosphere*, the land and the earth's climate interact closely with one another. The composition of the land both influences and is influenced by the weather in a region. In addition to this, human activities can affect and change the land, and therefore impact the weather and climate in an area.

Landmass

Landmass refers to a large area of land that is typically surrounded by an ocean or a sea. Continents and large islands are examples of landmasses. The earth has seven continents: North America, South America, Europe, Asia, Africa, Australia, and Antarctica. At one point in time, all of these continents were one large landmass known as a *supercontinent*. The name of this supercontinent is Pangaea. Over time, Pangaea broke into different pieces through a process known as **plate tectonics**. The pieces of the supercontinent eventually became our current continents.

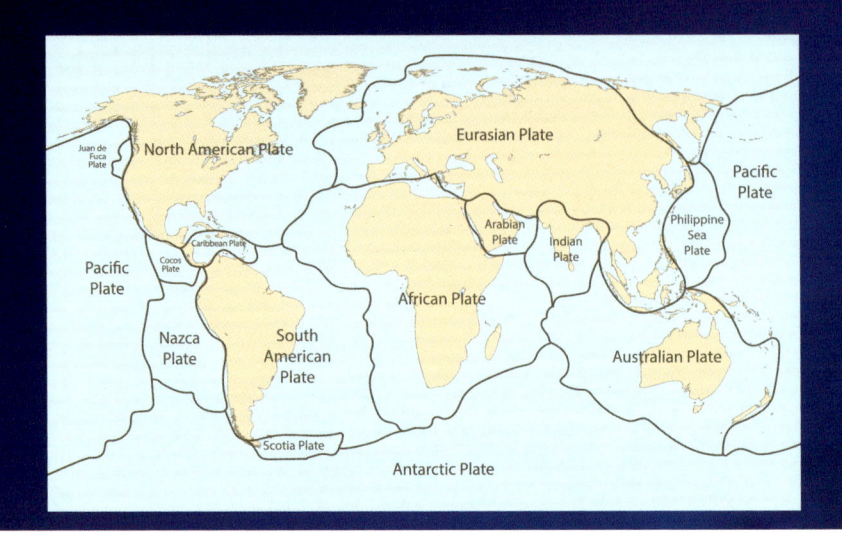

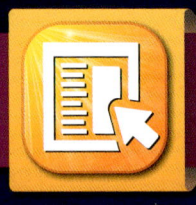

SUPERCONTINENTS

While Pangaea is the most widely known of the supercontinents, there have been other supercontinents throughout the earth's history. The oldest is thought to be Vaalbara, which probably existed around 3.6 billion years ago. The supercontinent of Ur formed around 3 billion years ago. Approximately 300 million years after Ur, Kenorlan formed. Then, 1.8 billion years later, the supercontinent of Colombia formed. Around 1.1 billion years ago, Rodinia was formed, followed by Pannotia, 100 million years after that. Pangaea followed, over 100 million years afterward.

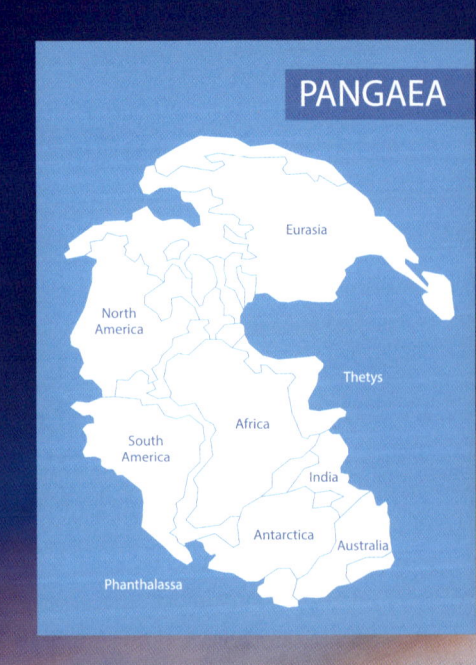

The New Weather: The Climate System

Landforms

Landforms are features that exist on the surface of the earth that are part of an area's terrain. There are four major types of landforms and four minor types of landforms. They are:

- **Mountains**
- **Hills**
- **Plateaus**
- **Plains**
- **Buttes**
- **Canyons**
- **Valleys**
- **Basins**

Mountains: Mountains are one of the four major types of landforms. They are elevated portions of the earth's **crust**, meaning they rise up above the rest of their surroundings. Mountains have steep slopes that lead up to a small summit.

Hills: The second kind of major landform are hills. Hills are areas of land that extend above the surrounding area. They aren't as high as mountains, and while they have a summit, the slopes of hills aren't as steep as slopes on mountains.

Plateaus: Plateaus, the third major landform, are elevated land masses that rise up sharply over an area on at least one side, sometimes as a steep slope and sometimes as vertical cliffs. The top of a plateau is usually very flat.

Plains: Plains consist of a flat stretch of land that usually stays near the same elevation throughout. There are very few trees in plain areas.

Buttes: Buttes are the first type of minor landform found on Earth. Buttes are tall towers of rock with steep sides and flat tops. They are typically isolated from other types of landforms and rise up from a flat area, such as a plain.

THE HIMALAYAS

Stretching across the northeastern part of India, the Himalayas are the highest mountain range in the world. Mount Everest is a part of the Himalayas. At 29,029 feet (8,848 m), it is the highest mountain peak in the world. This area is also known as the Third Pole. As the third largest deposit of snow and ice on the globe, it's an important part of the world's climate system. It is home to species such as the Bengal tiger, the one-horned rhinoceros, and the snow leopard.

Valleys: Valleys are long, low-lying areas that are usually located between mountains or hills. Most valleys have a river or stream running from one end of the valley to the other end.

The Moselle Valley covers northeastern France, southwestern Germany, and eastern Luxembourg. It is a beautiful region of the world and a popular tourist destination.

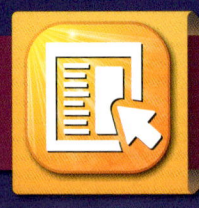

THE GRAND CANYON

Located in Arizona, the Grand Canyon is a large canyon encompassing 277 miles (446 km). At a mile deep (1.6 km) and up to 18 miles (29 km) wide, the oldest rocks in the Grand Canyon are an estimated to be 1.8 billion years old. The youngest layer of rock is 270 million years old. Colorado River has carved away at the rock of the Grand Canyon for around 5 or 6 million years. This means that the canyon itself is much younger than the rocks.

Basins: The fourth type of minor landform present on Earth are basins. These dips, located within the surface of the earth, have sides that are much higher than the bottom. Basins are circular or oval in shape, and some contain water.

Canyons: The second of the minor landforms, canyons are deep and narrow valleys that have very steep sides. They are formed by rivers cutting through rocky areas, weathering, erosion, and tectonic activities.

In Thingvellir National Park in Iceland, a person can stand on two continents at once. Imagine having one foot on the North American plate and the other on the Eurasian plate! These plates move about an inch (2.5 cm) apart each year, and have done so for millennia.

The Creation of Landmasses and Landforms

Landmasses and landforms are created over many thousands of years. According to the theory of plate tectonics, the earth's continents were once one giant landmass that gradually broke apart into different continents. The earth's crust is made up of various rock slabs (or plates) that slowly drift around on the surface of the earth. As the pieces drift apart, the force and friction caused by plates pulling away from and/or pushing into one another create new continents, as well as variety of landforms (topography) such as mountain ranges, volcanoes, and ocean ridges.

While some landforms were created via plate tectonics, others came about by the erosion of land through wind and water. Glaciers and ice sheets have also played an important role in carving out the topography across the world.

How Landmasses are Changing

Since changes in landmasses happen over lengthy periods of time, it can be difficult to see the changes. However, just as plate tectonics caused the formation of our current continents millions of years ago, these slabs of rock continue to slowly move today. It's estimated that tectonic plates move at a rate of one inch every year. There is some speculation that another supercontinent, like Pangaea, will one day form.

Recent studies conducted by scientists suggest that shifts in climate can lead to shifts in the earth's crust. This means that as our planet continues to warm, the speed of our tectonic plates' movement could increase, causing more volcanic eruptions, earthquakes, accelerating erosion, as well as causing new topography. Changing landscapes will also contribute to changes in weather and climate around the world.

Some studies also indicate that periods of **drought** can cause significant changes to the earth's crust. In 2017, researchers discovered that the Sierra Nevada mountain range rose by nearly

Kilauea in Hawaii is the world's most active volcano, followed by Etna in Italy, pictured above.

an inch when heavy precipitation arrived and filled the water catchments, and then fell by around half an inch due to the mountain's rocks losing water during a severe drought. These kind of changes might lead to additional seismic activity that could cause changes to our landscapes.

How Volcanoes Contribute to Landmass Changes

Volcanic activity is another contributing factor to landmass changes. When a volcano erupts, it violently releases molten rock (or **lava**) from deep inside of the earth. This causes new rock to form over the surface of the earth. As lava from the eruption gathers and cools on the earth's surface, it can form new landmasses.

A fairly rapid example of this is occurring on the coast of Tonga, where an island has appeared and disappeared several times throughout history. When a nearby volcano erupted around 1867, it led to the formation of a small island named Fonuafo'ou, meaning "New Land" in Tongan. An eruption in 1949 caused the island to fall in upon itself and disappear, and then it reformed in 2015.

In addition to having the ability to create new landmasses, volcanoes also have an impact on the earth's atmosphere. When eruptions occur, the carbon dioxide and other gases that stream from the volcano greatly influence the planet's climate. Global warming and climate change are both expected to contribute to the impact that these eruptions have on the planet. For example, a large-scale volcanic eruption that happens once or twice every 100 years could have a more-amplified impact on the climate than

Did you know that a volcanic eruption in 2014–2015 led to the creation of a small island? Watch this short video about this newly formed island.

56 The New Weather: The Climate System

VOLCANIC ERUPTIONS AND GREENHOUSE GASES

Volcanic eruptions tend to lead to periods of global cooling. However, the greenhouse gases that are emitted during an eruption enter the earth's atmosphere, where they can become trapped and contribute to increasing temperatures. When there are too many greenhouse gases in the atmosphere, they have no place to go, so they then cause the planet to warm. Therefore, volcanic activity can lead to the planet growing warmer over time. This is especially so when the planet is already experiencing a significant amount of warming.

it once would have had. Climate change will cause volcanic plumes to rise higher and spread faster around the planet, which will greatly amplify the cooling effect caused by volcanic eruptions.

Other research performed on volcanoes suggests that the number of volcanic eruptions that occur increases as glaciers melt. While scientists don't understand why this is the case, they believe that expanding glaciers place a great deal of pressure on the surface of the earth, which in turn impacts the way that magma flows. Once the glaciers have melted, that pressure will no longer be there and it'll be easier for magma to make its way to the earth's surface and cause a volcanic eruption.

How Humans are Changing Land Masses

Human beings can also significantly change the earth's surface. An example of this is through agriculture. In order to farm, people have to clear out forests. This has led to habitat loss in most areas, as well as soil erosion. Soil erosion is a serious problem, as it leads to a lack of nutrients for plants (including crops). It also leads to increased sedimentation and pollution in local waterways, such as rivers and stream. Soil erosion also contributes to extreme flooding. Experts believe that we have lost half of our planet's topsoil within the past 150 years.

Farming isn't the only way humans change land mass. Humans have also begun to construct artificial landmasses. For example, China has constructed artificial islands in the South China Sea. These islands were built on top of coral reefs or rocks. and have destroyed over 971 acres of coral reefs. There are still many reefs located in the immediate vicinity of these artificial islands, meaning that any accidents at sea could prove devastating to the remaining reefs. A similar project in the United Arab Emirates (UAE) is known as the *Palm Island Project*, the largest artificial island chain ever constructed. It has also had a significant impact on marine life and habitats in the area.

THE IMPORTANCE OF HEALTHY SOIL

Soil is a crucial part of our environment. Topsoil (the uppermost layer of soil) holds the nutrients necessary to sustain plant life. Having a healthy layer of topsoil means that we're better able to grow food. Over farming an area can lead to a loss of nutrients within the soil, which will impact entire ecosystems. This is why many farmers are beginning to pursue sustainable farming methods, which will preserve healthy topsoil so that we can continue to grow crops.

TEXT-DEPENDENT QUESTIONS

1. What is a landmass?
2. List the eight different types of landforms found on the earth.
3. Explain how volcanoes contribute to land mass changes

RESEARCH PROJECT

While artificially constructed islands help with human overpopulation and overcrowding concerns, they can do a great deal of harm to the environment. Conduct further research on the environmental impact of man-made islands. Using the information you gather, form your own opinion about whether construction of man-made islands should continue. Write a five-paragraph opinion paper explaining your position, using evidence to back up your argument. Share it with your science class.

WORDS TO UNDERSTAND

continental crust: the geologic layer of rocks that underlie the continents and the areas of shallow seabed close to their shores
density: the weight (or mass) of a substance per each unit volume
oceanic crust: the part of Earth's crust that makes up the seafloor; is thinner, denser, and simpler in structure than the continental crust
trenches: long, steep-sided valleys on the ocean floor

CHAPTER 5

OCEAN

The earth's ocean is the final component of the climate system. It stores heat from the sun, water, and carbon dioxide and carries them around the world while exchanging all of these resources with the earth's atmosphere. Ocean currents and circulation are also critical components of weather. You could say that the ocean and the atmosphere work together to form our weather and climate.

The ocean is a part of the hydrosphere element of the climate system. The hydrosphere is comprised of all of the water found on any planet. The six elements of the hydrosphere on Earth are:

- **Oceans**
- **Lakes**
- **Rivers**
- **Streams**
- **Ponds**
- **Groundwater**
- **Glaciers and Other Forms of Ice**

Imagine being the lighthouse keeper in the Petit Minou lighthouse! This picturesque structure is in Plouzane, France, on the westernmost point of the country and looking out into the Celtic Sea.

ONE OCEAN WITH MANY NAMES

The earth only has one ocean, but people have divided it into geographic areas and named them. Historically speaking, there were four: the Atlantic, the Pacific, the Indian, and the Arctic. However, in recent years most countries have begun to recognize a fifth: the Southern Antarctic.

Oceans: The earth's oceans are large bodies of saltwater that make up most of the surface of the earth.

Lakes: Lakes are large and deep bodies of water that are completely surrounded by land. They are usually fed by streams and rivers.

Rivers: Rivers are large streams of flowing water that are found all over the world. They flow toward oceans, seas, lakes, or other rivers.

Lakes like this one are abundant on Earth. This scenic lake is in Banff in the province of Alberta in Canada.

Ocean

Rivers and streams are important bodies of water on the earth. They flow toward oceans and are found all over the world.

Streams: Streams are a continuous body of surface water that flows within a channel. They usually feed into rivers, ponds, and lakes.

Ponds: Ponds are small bodies of freshwater that are surrounded by land. They are shallow and smaller than lakes. Ponds don't have any moving water.

Groundwater: Groundwater exists underneath the surface of the earth and is found within the cracks and spaces that exist in soil, sand, and rock. It eventually makes its way into streams, lakes, and oceans. Groundwater is an important part of our earth's water cycle.

Glaciers and Other Forms of Ice: Glaciers and other forms of ice are frozen water that exist in various locations around the world.

THE WATER CYCLE

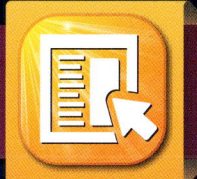

The water cycle is a process that explains how water exists and moves on, in, and above the earth. Water starts out as water vapor within the atmosphere that eventually falls from the sky in the form of precipitation. That precipitation filters into the ground until it reaches an area of groundwater, which then eventually makes its way into larger bodies of water. Water is then turned back into water vapor through the process of evaporation. From there, the entire cycle starts over again.

The Earth's Ocean Mass

The ocean accounts for approximately 71 percent of the earth's surface. Approximately 61 percent of the Northern Hemisphere is comprised of ocean, while 80 percent of the Southern Hemisphere is made up of ocean. Around 97 percent of all of the water in the world is in the ocean. Although the ocean makes up such a large portion of our planet, we've only explored around 20 percent of it. In fact, we've explored and mapped out more of the moon and the planet Mars than we have our own ocean.

While there are many mysteries surrounding our ocean, we do know that it contains mountain ranges and canyons (called **trenches**), just like the ones on land. There are also around 226,000 species of marine plants and animals that live in the ocean. Scientists believe that approximately 90 percent of the ocean's species are still yet to be discovered. As you can see, the ocean is a vast expanse of water that still has many secrets for us to uncover.

A History of Oceans on Earth

Billions of years ago, when the earth originated, the planet produced so much heat that it was a molten planet. Due to this, the materials that make up the planet settled depending on their **density**. During these early years of Earth's geological history, these denser materials moved toward the center of the planet, becoming its core, while the lighter materials flowed near the top, becoming the crust. There are two different types of crust on Earth—**continental crust** and **oceanic crust**.

For a long period of time, water remained in a gaseous state. Around 3.8 billion years ago, the earth's temperature cooled to below 212°F (100 °C), which caused water vapor and other types of gases to escape from the planet. Once the surface of the earth cooled down enough, rain was able to fall. This rain fell for several hundred years and drained into the hollows formed within the planet's surface. This water is what became our ocean.

As the earth's shifting plates continued to collide, push, and create friction against one another, geological features such as canyons and mountain ranges began to form in the ocean, just as they did on land. This process took billions of years to occur.

Around 2.5 billion years ago, enough oxygen became present within the earth's atmosphere for life to form and be supported by the planet. The theory of evolution states that these first forms of life were single-celled microbes that lived within the ocean. More complicated multi-celled life evolved around 1.2 billion years ago. All of these life forms evolved in the ocean, and eventually found their way to land.

Throughout the earth's history, the ocean has been home to millions of creatures, sustaining life both within it and outside of it. Today, humans rely on oceans for food, trade, and industry. And since it has such an important part to play in the development of our weather and climate, we also rely on it as a part of our climate system.

Are Oceans Changing?

As the climate on Earth grows warmer and the climate gradually changes, the oceans are also experiencing a great deal of transformation. One of the most telling indicators of these changes are rising sea levels. Since 1880, the ocean has risen at a rate of six-tenths of an inch every ten years. However, in recent years, this rise in sea levels has increased to over an inch every decade.

The ocean is also getting warmer. Each of the earth's oceans have experienced rapidly warming temperatures since the 1990s. In fact, the year 2021 was the warmest recorded year for ocean temperatures. This is one of the contributing factors toward rising sea levels and melting sea ice. It's also one of the reasons why

TRILOBITES

Around 540 million years ago, the Cambrian Period saw the emergence of trilobites. These creatures are perhaps the most famous ones to emerge from this period, and are closely related to the crabs, spiders, and insects that we see today. These creatures had segmented bodies and came in interesting shapes and sizes. In fact, scientists estimate that there were more than 20,000 trilobite species. They spent their time moving across the ocean floor and catching food.

Arctinurus boltoni is a type of trilobite species. The adult trilobites reached about eight inches in length and lived in deep water in semitropical regions.

tropical storms and hurricanes are growing larger and lasting for longer periods of time.

Another way that the earth's oceans are changing is that its chemistry is becoming more acidic. Since 1850, the acidity of the oceans has risen by 26 percent, which is ten times faster than it rose at any time within the past 55 million years. This modification in acidity levels impact marine life, threaten food security, and could lead to the loss of jobs due to a lack of tourism, fishing, or other industries related to the ocean. In addition to this, the more acidic the ocean becomes, the less carbon dioxide it will be able to absorb. More CO_2 will remain in the atmosphere, causing an increase in global warming temperatures.

As these changes in the ocean continue, they pose a great danger to coral reefs, which harbor an abundance of marine life. As coral reefs are damaged and destroyed due to acidic waters and rising temperatures, the life contained within them will also die off. This not only impacts marine life, but it will also negatively affect the livelihoods of those living in areas that rely on fishing, tourism, and other related industries that need the coral reefs in order to survive.

Due to changes in the ocean, many marine species are migrating away from areas where they once lived. Several species of whales have had to change some of their migration and mating patterns due to a lack of food in areas such as the Arctic. A lack of zooplankton fed by warm waters have caused Atlantic cod to migrate to different areas. This has had a significant impact on local fisheries in the Northeast United States.

The Ocean and Climate Change

As we discussed earlier in this chapter, the ocean acts as storage for heat from the sun, as well as for carbon dioxide. As CO_2 emissions have continued to rise because of human activity, the ocean has absorbed many of these emissions. This is why the ocean has become more acidic over the past several decades. And as the planet continues to warm, the ocean will continue storing that heat, leading to a decrease in marine life, melting sea ice, melting polar ice caps, and rising sea levels.

The scientific consensus is that our current trend of global warming and climate change is caused primarily by human activities. Reducing our carbon dioxide and greenhouse gas emissions will help us to maintain our oceans, as well as slow down the impact of global climate change.

Scan here to view a short video about how climate change is affecting our oceans.

TEXT-DEPENDENT QUESTIONS

1. List the elements of the hydrosphere.
2. How much of the earth's surface is made up of the ocean?
3. In what ways are our oceans changing?

RESEARCH PROJECT

Most scientists agree that human activities are the primary cause of climate change and global warming. The condition of our oceans is one of the primary pieces of evidence of this. Using the library and the internet, conduct research on how climate change impacts our oceans. Write an informative article about the topic, including a section on how human activities have contributed to this, and share it with your weather club.

SERIES GLOSSARY OF KEY TERMS

alpine: relating to high mountains, including living or growing on mountains above the tree line.

biomes: the types of animals and plants that live within a particular habitat.

continental crust: the geologic layer of rocks that underlie the continents and the areas of shallow seabed close to their shores.

crust: the outmost layer of the earth that is made up of different kinds of rocks.

density: the weight (or mass) of a substance per each unit volume.

drought: a prolonged dry period that can cause extensive crop damage and limit drinking water for humans and animals.

ecosystems: localized communities of organisms that interact amongst themselves and their physical environments.

epoch: the smallest measurement of geological time.

extinction: the elimination of a species, family, or other group of plant or animal from existence.

humidity: the amount of water vapor that is found in the air

jet stream: a fast flowing, narrow, meandering river of wind in the earth's atmosphere.

lava: molten rock ejected from a volcano during an eruption; the same name is applied to the rock when cooled and hardened.

natural habitat: an environmental area where a specific species lives and calls home.

oceanic crust: the part of Earth's crust that makes up the seafloor; is thinner, denser, and simpler in structure than the continental crust.

plate tectonics: a theory accepted by the scientific community that states that the earth is made of giant slabs of solid rock that move slowly and change the structure of the earth.

sea level: the average height of the ocean's surface.

snowpack: the amount of accumulating snow in a season in a mountainous area.

trenches: long, steep-sided valleys on the ocean floor.

ultraviolet (UV) radiation: a type of electromagnetic radiation that is present in sunlight.

FURTHER READING AND INTERNET RESOURCES

BOOKS

Ervin-Blankenheim, Elisabeth. *Song of the Earth: Understanding Geology and Why it Matters.* New York, NY: Oxford University Press, 2021.

Herman, Gail. *What is Climate Change?* New York, NY: Penguin Random House, 2018.

Medina, Nico. *What Was the Ice Age?* New York, NY: Penguin Random House, 2017.

Shofner, Melissa Rae. *Understanding Earth's Systems: Earth's Atmosphere.* New York, NY: PowerKids Press, 2018.

Smith, Richard. *The World Beneath: The Life and Times of Unknown Sea Creatures and Coral Reefs.* New York, NY: Apollo Publishers, 2019.

WEBSITES

EPA Climate Change Resources for Educators and Students
https://www.epa.gov/climate-change/climate-change-resources-educators-and-students

A compilation of resources about climate change provided by the United States Environmental Protection Agency.

The MarineBio Conservation Society
https://www.marinebio.org/

This website of the MarineBio Conservation Society includes an abundance of resources on marine biology and climate change.

NASA's Eyes on the Earth
https://eyes.jpl.nasa.gov/eyes-on-the-earth.html

An app that allows you to monitor the vital signs of the planet.

PBS Learning Media
https://rmpbs.pbslearningmedia.org/subjects/science/earth-and-space-science/earths-atmosphere/

A collection of resources on earth science and space science from PBS.

ORGANIZATIONS TO CONTACT

National Oceanic and Atmospheric Administration
1401 Constitution Avenue NW, Room 5128
Washington, DC 20230
Website: https://www.noaa.gov

National Weather Service
NWS Education
1325 East West Highway
Silver Spring, MD 20910
Website: https://www.weather.gov

US Environmental Protection Agency
1200 Pennsylvania Avenue, NW
Washington, DC 20460
Phone: (202) 564-4700
Website: https://www.epa.gov

The Water Research Foundation
6666 West Quincy Avenue
Denver, CO 80235
Website: https://www.waterrf.org

INDEX

A
Africa, 47
agricultural activities, 26, 57–58
air pollution, 28
Alaska, 20
Alberta, 63
Amazon rain forest, 25
Andean-Saharan ice age, 37
animals, 26
Antarctica
   desert, 18
   discussion, 47
   ice, 33
   ice shelves, 36
   ozone hole, 10
   research stations, 44
Arctic ocean, 62
Arctic Pole, 33, 36
artificial biospheres, 28–29, 33
artificial islands, 64–65
Asia, 47
Atlantic ocean, 62
atmosphere
   atmosphere, 13–17
   CO_2, 18
   discussion, 6–8
   layers, 8–12
   ozone gas, 13–17
   smog, 12–13
   UV radiation and, 6, 8, 13, 15
aurora borealis, 11
Australia, 47

B
Banff (Canada), 63
basins, 59
biomes, 20, 78
biosphere
   artificial, 28–29, 33
   deforestation and, 34–36
   discussion, 20–21, 30, 32
   maintaining health of, 32, 34
   parts of, 21–27
buttes, 55

C
Canada, 63
canyons, 58–59
carbon dioxide (CO_2)
   deforestation and, 34–36
   discussion, 18
   photosynthesis and, 30
   rising sea levels and, 69–70
   volcanoes and, 62
carbon emissions, 18, 30, 32
China, 58

climate change
   biosphere and, 30, 32
   discussion, 7–8
   global warming versus, 17
   human activities and, 32, 63–64, 69–70
   oceans and, 69–70
   volcanoes and, 62–63
closed life-support systems, 28–29, 33
Colombia supercontinent, 48
Colorado River, 52
conservation, 32, 34
continental crust, 64, 66, 72, 78
continents, 53
coral reefs, 64, 75
crust
   continental, 64, 66, 72, 78
   discussion, 52, 55, 78
   oceanic, 66, 72, 79
Cryogenian ice age, 37
cryosphere
   discussion, 38–39, 41–44
   Earth's health and, 46, 48–50
   ice ages, 43–44
   sea level and, 49

D
deciduous forests, 22, 26
deforestation, 34–36
deserts, 22, 24
droughts, 52, 60–61, 78

E
ecosphere. *See* biosphere
ecosystems, 20, 72
electromagnetic radiation, 6
Environmental Protection Agency, 76
EPA Climate Change Resources, 76
epochs, 38, 43, 78
Ervin-Blankenheim, Elisabeth, 74
Etna, 55
Eurasian plate, 53
Europe, 34, 53
evolution, 73
exosphere, 9, 11
extinction, 20, 36, 47, 78

F
factories, 32
farming
   climate change and, 32
   landmasses and, 63–64
fishing, 32, 34, 75
flooding
   discussion, 49–50
   soil erosion and, 63–64
Fonuafo'ou, 56

Index

INDEX

forests
    deciduous, 22, 26
    deforestation and, 34–36
    tropical rain, 22, 25
fossil fuels, 18
France, 62
fresh water, 42, 49–50
frozen ground, 39, 41, 43

G
Geological Time Scale, 39
glaciers
    discussion, 39, 41–42, 50, 61, 64
    landforms and, 60
    shrinking of, 48
    water cycle and, 65
global warming
    discussion, 17
    human activities and, 32, 63–64, 69–70
    volcanoes and, 62–63
Grand Canyon, 52
greenhouse gases, 62–63
Greenland, 36
ground-level ozone, 13
groundwater, 67, 70–71

H
Hawaii, 61
Herman, Gail, 74
hills, 55
Himalayas, 50
history, 66–68
Holocene epoch, 37
human activities, 32, 63–64, 69–70
humidity, 38, 41
Huronian ice age, 43
hydrosphere
    changes to, 74–75
    climate change and, 69–70
    discussion, 22, 27, 60–66
    history of, 66-68
    water cycle and, 71

I
ice
    discussion, 38–39, 41–44, 67, 70
    Earth's health and, 46, 48–50
    water cycle and, 71
ice ages, 43–44
icebergs, 39, 41
ice caps, 39, 50
ice cores, 41, 46
Iceland, 42, 46, 59
ice sheets, 39, 42, 60
ice shelves, 39, 41–42
Indian ocean, 68
interglacial periods, 43–44
International Center for Closed Ecosystems, 23
ionosphere, 9, 12

islands, 62, 64–65
Italy, 61

J
jet stream, 6, 10, 72

K
Karoo ice age, 43
Kenorlan supercontinent, 54
Kilauea, 61

L
lakes, 67, 69, 71
land, 52–54
landforms, 55–60
land management, 32, 34
landmasses
    changing of, 60–61
    creation of, 60
    human activities and, 63–64
    types of, 53–54
    volcanoes and, 61–63
lava, 52, 61, 72
lithosphere
    artificial islands, 65
    discussion, 52–53
    human activities and, 63–64
    landforms, 55–60
    land management, 32, 34
    landmasses, 53–54, 60–61
    supercontinents, 54
    volcanoes and, 61–63

M
man-made changes, 32, 63–64, 69–70
MarineBio Conservation Society, 75
Mars, 27
McMurdo Station (Antarctica), 44
Medina, Nico, 74
mesosphere, 9–10
methane gas, 32
Moselle Valley, 51
mountains, 38, 55

N
NASA, 42, 75
National Oceanic and Atmospheric Administration, 76
National Snow and Ice Data Center, 44, 50
National Weather Service, 76
natural habitats, 20, 32, 72
North America, 26, 50, 53, 59
northern lights, 11
North Pole, 33

O
oceanic crust, 66, 72, 73
oceans
    acidity, 69-70
    changes to, 69–70
    climate change and, 69–70
    discussion, 22, 27, 60–66

history of, 66–68
rising level of, 69–70
water cycle and, 65
over farming, 32, 63–64
overfishing, 32, 34
overhunting, 34
oxygen, 30, 72–73
ozone-depleting substances (ODS), 10
ozone gas, 12–17
ozone hole, 15–16

P

Pacific ocean, 68
Palm Island Project, 64
Pangaea supercontinent, 53–54, 60
Pannotia supercontinent, 54
PBS Learning Media, 75
permafrost, 39, 44
Petit Minou lighthouse, 62
photosynthesis, 30
plains, 55
plateaus, 55
plate tectonics
discussion, 52–53, 60, 73
landforms, 55–59
landforms and, 60
landmasses and, 53–54, 60–61
volcanoes and, 61–63
poles, 39, 42
pollution, 12–13, 32, 34
ponds, 61, 70–71
power plants, 32
prairies, 22–23
precipitation, 6–7. *See also specific forms of precipitation*

Q

QR Videos
aurora borealis, 11
climate change and oceans, 70
deforestation, 36
major ice ages, 44
volcanic island creation, 62
Quaternary ice age, 43

R

renewable energy, 9, 34
research project
on artificial island-creation, 65
average snowfall rates, 51
biosphere in a bottle, 37
climate change and oceans, 70
on layers of atmosphere, 19
research stations, 50
rivers, 67, 69–71
Rodinia supercontinent, 48

S

sea ice, 39, 41, 49

sea level
discussion, 6, 9, 50, 73
gradual rise in, 68–69
Smith, Richard, 68
smog, 12–13
snow, 38–39, 41
snowpack, 38, 50, 73
soil, 36, 64
soil erosion, 63–64
solar power, 9–10
solar radiation, 6, 8, 39, 48
Song of the Earth (Ervin-Blankenheim), 74
South America, 53
South China Sea, 58
Southern Antarctic ocean, 62
southern lights, 11
South Pole, 39–40, 42
stratosphere, 9–10, 13, 15–16
streams, 67, 70–71
supercontinents, 53–54, 60
sustainability, 32, 34, 63–64

T

thermosphere, 9, 11
The World Beneath (Smith), 74
Thingvellir National Park (Iceland), 53
Tonga, 56
topsoil
deforestation and, 36
discussion, 32, 34, 64
soil erosion and, 63–64
trenches, 66, 72, 73
trilobites, 73, 74
tropical rain forests, 22, 25
troposphere, 9
tundras, 22

U

ultraviolet (UV) radiation
discussion, 6, 8, 14, 73
ozone gas and, 13, 15
Understanding Earth's Systems (Shofner, Melissa Rae), 74
United Arab Emirates (UAE), 58
Ur supercontinent, 54

V

Vaalbara supercontinent, 54
valleys, 57
vehicles, 32
volcanoes, 61–63

W

water cycle, 70–71
Water Research Foundation, 76
weather, 7–8
Western Europe, 34
What Is Climate Change? (Herman), 74
What Was the Ice Age (Medina), 74
wildfires, 32

Index 79

AUTHOR'S BIOGRAPHY

HEATHER PIDCOCK-REED holds a master's degree in professional writing from Chatham University, where she studied topics such as science and environmental writing, political and news writing, and technical writing. Other titles by Heather include *Contemporary Civil Rights Issues: The Environment and Immigration,* and the Living with Dogs series. Heather currently resides in La Junta, Colorado.

PHOTO CREDITS

All images in this book are in the public domain or have been supplied under license by © Shutterstock.com. The publisher credits the following images as follows:
Page: 6 Julius Silver, 8 Arek Ssocha, 10 Samuel Faber, 13 city-4772482 Admiral Lebioda, 14 P. Artsiom, 18 Lori Lo, 20 David Mark, 21 tonxijesse, 23 Joshua Woroniecki, 24 Peter H, 25 Máté Markovics, 26 Bhargava Marripati, 27 University of Arizona, 28 Marc Pascual, 29 biospherefoundation.org, 31 Robert Jones, 34 Pexels, 36 David Mark, 37 Nico Grutter, 40 Erebor Mountain, 41 J. Plenio, 43 Andrea Spallanzani, 46 Aline Dassel, 48 kalonko and tinkivinki, 50 truthseeker08, 51 Peter H, 52 Hardeback Media, 53 DL, 55 Sony Ilce, 60 Joakant, 62 David Mark, 63 James Wheeler, 64 Jorg Vieli, 65 Artisticco, 68 Wikimedia Images